EMBRACE MY PASSION

2ND EDITION

Inspiring Poems/Pictures/Journal
By
Ayana Johnson/Empress Yana Jay

DEDICATION

This book is dedicated to my beautiful daughter Aanaya "BK" Frank. The moment you came into my life I was never the same. Thank you Aanaya for making me a better person on the inside and out. I am so proud to be your mother!

Also, in loving memories of everyone who has made a huge impact in my life like, Martha McGualey-Stewart, Edna Mae Johnson, Willie Mae Miller (Madear), Sarah Evans, Jessie Miller, Sherri Baker, Ayanna Wesley, Jekokni Baker, Joseph Thomas.

COME GO WITH ME PRECIOUS QUEEN!

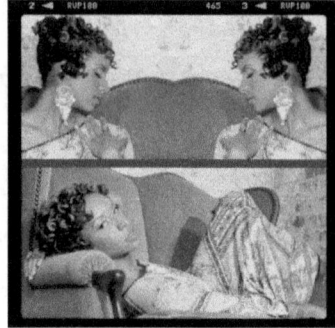

From my heart to yours! I am blessed to share a collection of motivating poems, photos and journal writing for women all over the world. I offer a light of love within all the confusion. May this book generate new ideas and help you walk with your head higher in this world. With so many negative images of women on the television and disrespectful lyrics on the radio, may this book offer a breath of fresh air to your mind and help you grow toward your dreams and goals. Follow your bliss and continue to follow your dreams. Read! Share! Give us feedback at: Empresslyfe.com

Being a lady is cool! Celebrate your womanhood today and every day! EMBRACE MY PASSION!!!

TABLE OF CONTENTS

"Born in America" 6
"Naala" 8
"Why are you asking me? 11
"Searching" 14
"Princess in training" 16
"Hard Times" 17
"Wake Up" 19
"Third Eye Vision" 20
"Observing" 21
"Enlighten Your Mind" 24
"Soft Kisses" 27
""Storm"28
Starting Over" 29
"Cease the Curse" 30
"Unprotected Thunder" 33
"Caller I.D." 36
"My Reflection" 37

"BORN IN AMERICA"

(An elderly lady observes a young boy from her front
window)
Excuse me little one but where are you going?
You should cover your head
Because it's cold outside and snowing
I see you walking by
Walking the streets with your head down
Why can't you lift your head when I am talking to
you?
What is so interesting on the ground?
(& he looked up to her and said)
I'm glad that you stopped me
Cause my mind is in a race
I'm confused about MY soul's final resting place
In school I learned that the KKK were true devoted
Christians
Taken over this country and killing MY ancestors was
their mission? I also read that if my ancestors were
caught
Reading anything other than a BIBLE
THEY WERE KILLED!
But now I am supposed to go to this same church
and be HEALED?
They found many innocent African men hanging
from that same cross
Yet this is the same religion that saves many souls
from being lost?

(A tear drops from his eye)
I can't even imagine what my ancestors suffered
Or feel their pain
I keep questioning my parents
Wondering if my prayers are in vain
There are so many GOD's
How do you know whom to choose?
Jesus, Buddha, Ja or should I just change my name to
Muhammad-Abdul
So, yes you see I am walking
Searching for the truth
Indeed thank you ma'am for stopping me
At least someone cares about the young black youth.

"NAALA"

Puzzles of constant uniform bridges cross my
sight
T.V. shows me seventeen deaths in one night
My parents can't relate
Schools bring unsafe fright
Limitless distractions keep me inferior in your
sight
INDEED I AM YOUR REFLECTION
It would be at your discretion to hold tight
Combine
Contort
Your way through my tunnel until there was light
Why do we listen to lyrics of such strife?
Slapping hoes
Shake that ass
Cheat on your wife?
Famous fools with no insight!
Children can't see you working hard
Still money is tight
What they do see are the iced out chains, big
booty girls and the Lexus cars
That appear right
They wanna be the next player
#1 stunner
PIMP TIGHT!
Achieve to capture their attention without the
glamour life

They have to know that THE MOST HIGH is first in the real world
That television won't teach them to live right.

Freestyle! Write about whatever comes to your mind. Go!

_____

_____

_____

_____

_____

_____

_____

_____

_____

_____

_____

_____

_____

_____

_____

_____

_____

_____

_____

_____

_____

_____

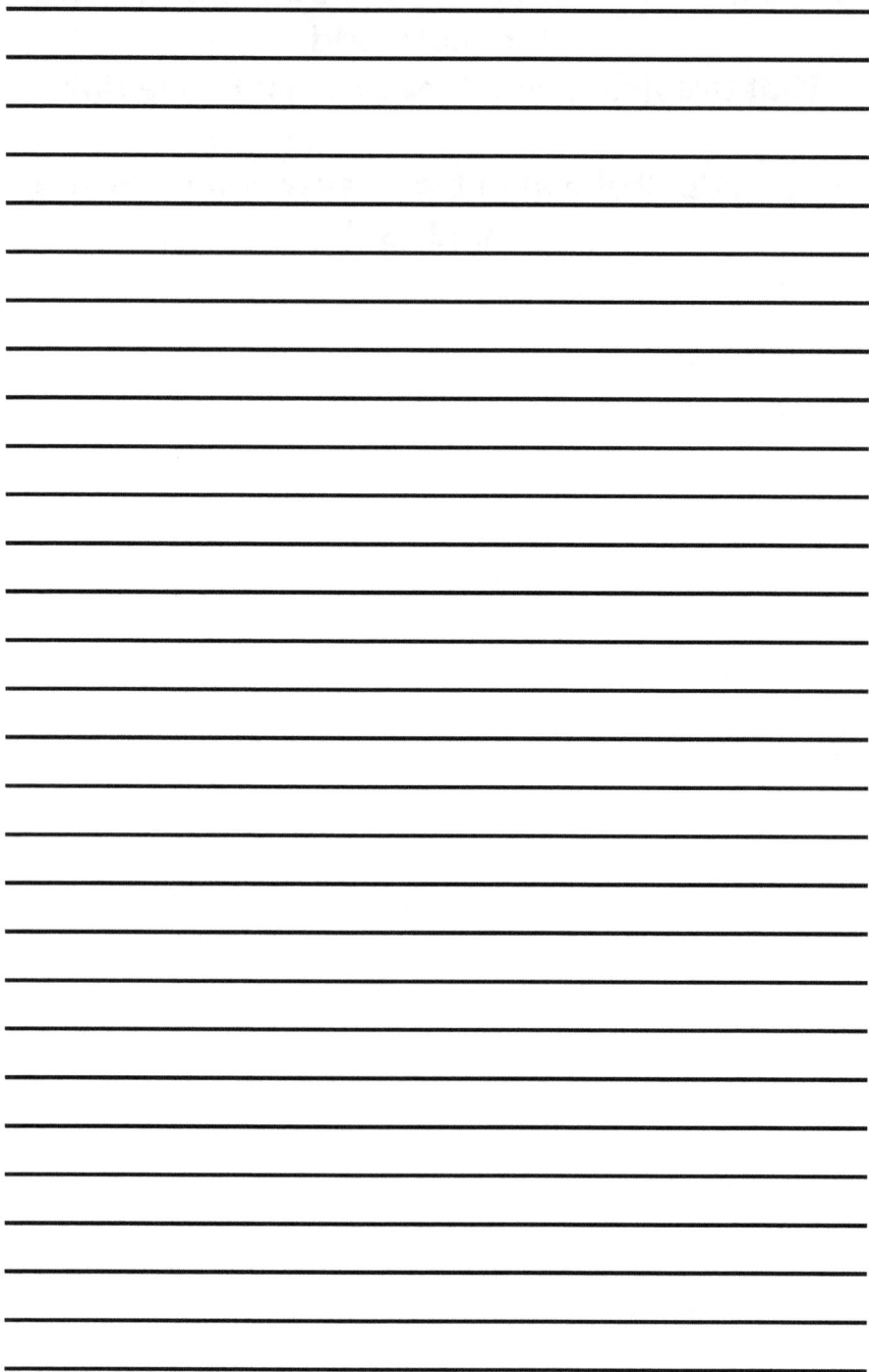

Why are you asking me???

Is it wrong to do what I feel?
Or am I dreaming of things that never will?
Did the BIBLE just happen?
Or is it all a form of control?
Will time reveal the truth when I am grey and old?
Why are there 20 churches and 35 liquor stores in my community?
My people work hard to make YOU RICH and WE NEED EQUALITY?
Is church a business now?
How you go from playa rapper to pastor?
How can I motivate the young ones?
What made them call you master?
Why are the beautiful ones hated?
If so, why does everyone want beauty?
Why do we kill unborn babies?
Why do you wait for someone else to treat you like a lady?
How do single mothers work so hard and get little respect?
Why do I see my little Goddesses walking around with "SEXY: tattooed on their neck?
Why do men love and leave with no regret?
Why do women pretend not to love?
Why is a PIMP someone glorified to be?

What is really in the sky above?
Is it me?
Or are you tired of T.V.?

Write a poem about what you are tired of seeing
daily on T.V.

_____

_____

_____

_____

_____

_____

_____

_____

_____

_____

_____

_____

_____

_____

_____

_____

_____

_____

_____

_____

_____

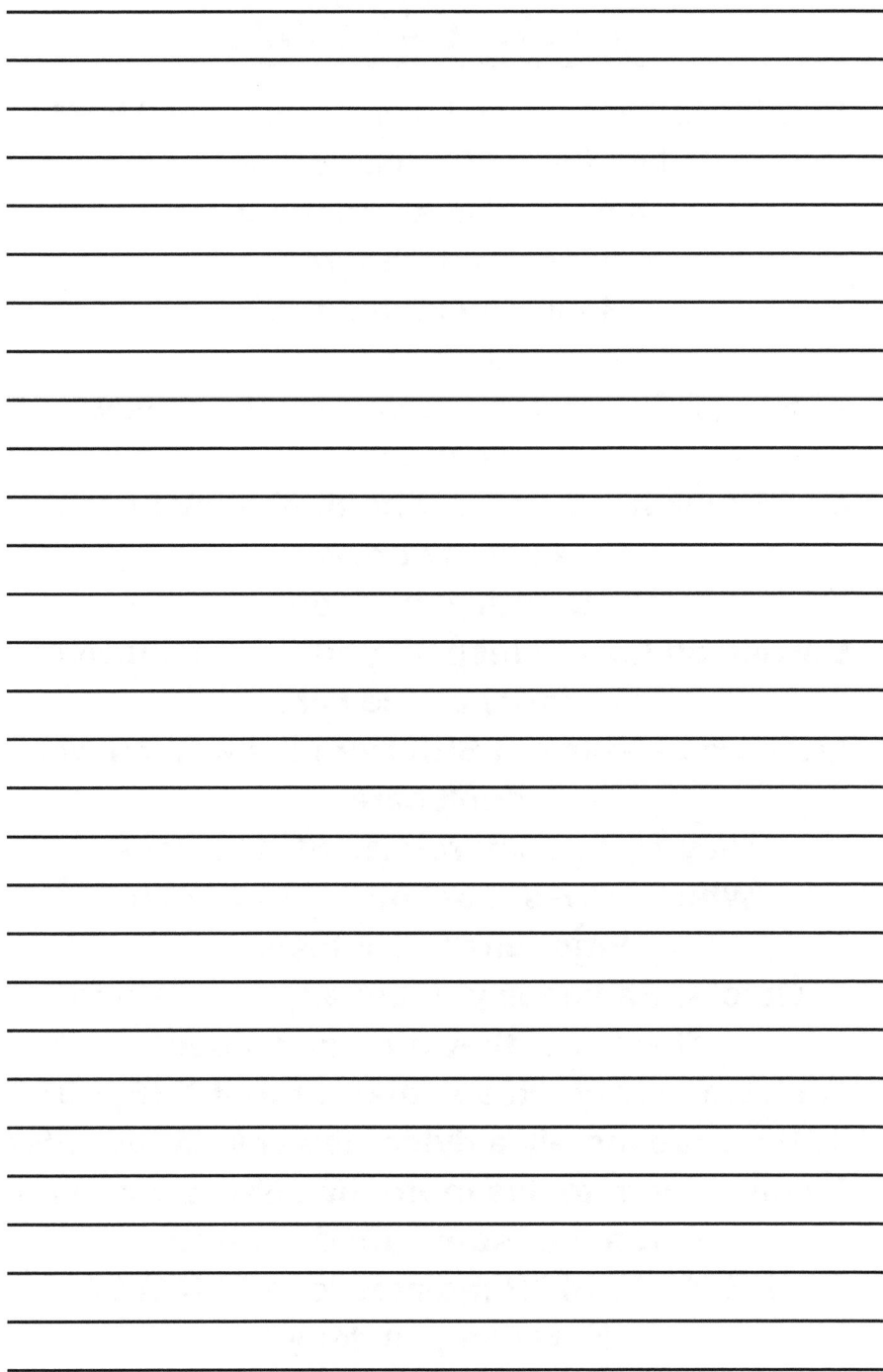

"Searching"

Wind flies past me as I wonder what will begin
Is it the end or beginning?
This world is so confusing
I can't seem to figure it out
Hmmmmmmmmmm?
Let's see
MONEY, POWER, LIES & SEX is what this world
is about
MONEY moves the men who think they have the
almighty power
But they are fools
Unwise on how to respect you and themselves
Majority are cowards
LIES are used to get SEX from the women who
don't care
They try to compromise SEX for love
Which leaves most men and women
Emotionally confused
Quick-SEX keeps you unhappy and alone
Therefore, they are being used
I wish we only could see that without THE MOST
HIGH we are merely a dying flower without water
We must learn to use more than 5% of our mind
before our souls are devoured
THE MOST HIGH radiates love FOREVER
How can you deny?

This is the kind of love that I want in my life
The kind of love I'll choose over any guy
THE MOST HIGH has always been there
Always by my side
Still I become so selfish that I push the love aside
Living in a world like this
Why should I stand out?
Why should I try?
And as I sit here with the wind still passing me by
I look up at the sky and ask myself
WHY?

Empress Yana Jay in Jamaica, Montego Bay

"Princess in Training"

Poetry helps me heal
It helps me unravel
All the emotions that I hide
Maybe I should call it a GOD given prize?
The older I become
The more I see
Godly ways inside me
Those are naturally
Re-adjusting in and out of reality
Looking in the mirror
Not knowing if that's me!
Always catching a baby in a smile
Going out of my way to make it worth your while
After you are happy
What's next?
My mind?
Always PROTECT!
Was raised with much respect
Can't stand money hungry platinum chains
Always on the flex
My beauty beats rapidly
Behind the ribs in my chest
My lips and words have created where I stand
NOW WHO YOU WAN COME TEST?!?!?

"HARD TIMES"

These are hard times
I talk in my sleep to ease the stress on my mind
Driving past Magic City
I see the same old thang
Little girl
Short skirt
Tryna come up on some change
The older I become
The more I see
GODLY WAYS INSIDE ME
Those are naturally
SICK of WACK MC's
WHO LABEL ME?
FREAK, HOE, SLUT
YO! That's insanity!
You see
Love is more deeper than passion
Most girls think they can find it
In men and cash and
Never realizing material status
NEVER LAST
And he's long gone
Now you're showing another man your thong
SO START LOVING YOURSELF GIRL!
You'll never go wrong!
I move with precise
Locs

Legs Wedges be nice
I'm a rock and rip the runway
Living my life
Killing'em in cheetah print
Ain't no need for the ice
Yeah Romney did try
Obama doing it twice
U-N-I-T-Y Latifah said it best
U-N-I-T-Y
Cause I wish a fella would
I WISH A FELLA WOULD
I gotta get this off my chest
I wish a fella would
Play me like a freak
My hustle is so Russell
My swagga is so unique
I WISH A FELLA WOULD
Play me?
Like a trick
Po pimp riding round
In my whip ACTING RICH!?!?!?

"Wake Up"

Yo, when I wrote this
I wrote to preach
Reach your brain
I wanna help you maintain ladies
Open leg man after man brings eternal pain
Giving up yourself for money is INSANE
If you took time to love yourself
You'd realize what you have
They don't love you
Disrespect you!
That's basic math
Some fool you with the bling bling
And tons of cash
Yo, these songs of men deceiving women
Sound more like psychopaths
Never will I give what is holy
To trash
In the end you are stuck by yourself to face the
aftermath.

"Third Eye Vision"

My mission completed
Your soul is deleted
I speak that realness
My foes feel defeated
My thoughts are quick don't trip
They can't be repeated
Red eye men try to play me!
Then on my back you want to lay me?
PLEASE!!! I'm on a mission!
Keeping many wishing
I bleed emotions from my pen
Can you handle the competition?
Quick to hate but still my book you bought!
You can't stop
You won't stop.
I got your eyes locked
and your mind in a daze
They call it braids in a maze
Are these the last days?
Sex addict
Dope fiend
I'm rising chasing dreams
Before I listen to this clown
Tryna sell me a dream?????

'Observing'

Words are seeds that surrounds us in the air on
the walls
Different languages
Various meanings
Reverse your thoughts
Allowing insecure judgments to fall
Enjoying common eye contact may lead to
inquire
Joyful conversation that few admire
Have you ever thought about what sparks a
conversation?
What is she/he living for?
Linked hearts and cherished reputations waiting
behind that door
The KEY is your heart and self-love.
In which you search outside yourself.
Hidden pictures of tedious ways to reach the
highest wealth
Family and friends are pushed aside
For green paper that is touched my million men
Quick! Catch me! Grab me!
Stand
Hold on to me forever
However
My feet is in quick sad.

Poem challenge! Write about your future. Go!

_____

_____

_____

_____

_____

_____

_____

_____

_____

_____

_____

_____

_____

_____

_____

_____

_____

_____

_____

_____

_____

_____

_____

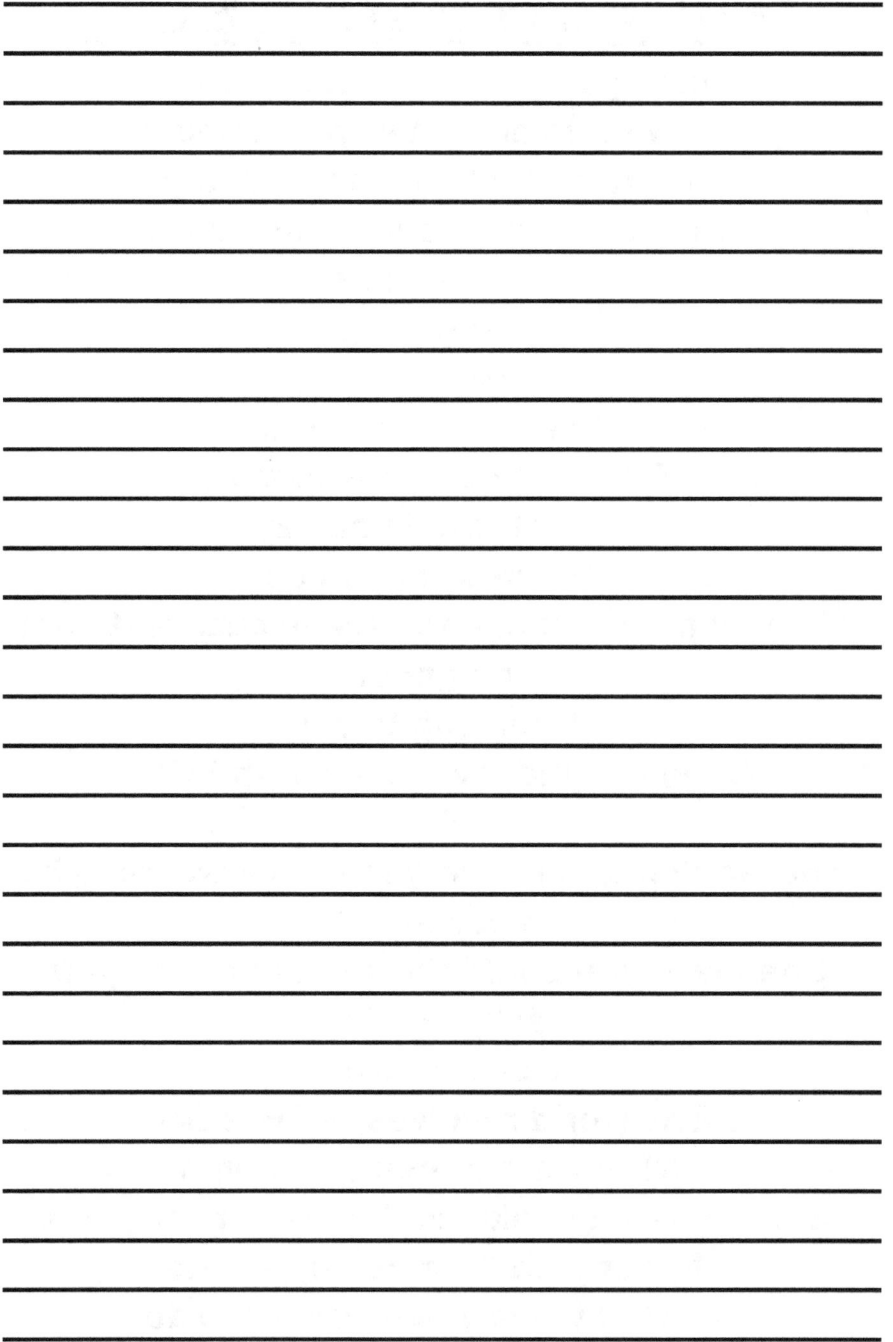

"ENLIGHTEN YOUR MIND"

Come go with me precious Queen
I want to enlighten your mind
I want to teach you a few things
Life is not all about being a dime
Luxury cars
Bling bling
Meditate
Get your mind right
Choose your OWN destiny
Watch what you say
Watch what you do
It's only natural that baby sis, lil cuz, next door
neighbor
Looks up to you
Respect and love starts with YOU!
NO!
You won't find it in every man that wants to be
your friend
One place you could find yourself is on your
back, legs high
Ready to give in
The world revolves WITHIN US
WE have the precious womb
Stop pretending like all the fussing, arguing,
fighting on them reality shows
is what you always wanted to do
You know that mindset is doomed

No one will recognize that you are a jewel
Pure wisdom
Until you recognize it yourself
Tired of our women exploiting themselves in
these videos
Lyrics saying how you will lay down for his
wealth
So STOP!
BREATHE!
THINK!
BE SMART!
TAKE CARE OF YOURSELF!

Write a poem about you taking care of your life, mind and body.

_____

_____

_____

_____

_____

_____

_____

_____

_____

_____

_____

_____

_____

_____

_____

_____

_____

_____

_____

_____

_____

_____

_____

_____

"Soft Kisses"

Darling, you are beautiful
Stand tall
You peace seeking KING
Yes, I claim you as my own
Without the material ring
Outsiders may view you as a thug
Criminal selling green
But that is just foolish
They ONLY assume
They can't begin to understand why your face
looks mean
They constantly racial profile you
Try to fit you into the new crime scene
But I stand beside you brother
Until the end
Indeed YOU ARE MY KING
Yes, I claim you as my own without the material
ring
We share veins of blood that screams for equality
in this world
We share what is unseen!

"Storm"

Thunder awakes me out of my sleep
I walk slowly to the window to take a quick peep
The sky looks so perfect
The air feels so still
Living and eating for two
My spirit is free to do whatever at will
My husband is still asleep
My son is too
But this thunder keeps waking me up and it's a
quarter past two
Trees start to sway
As I toss and turn in my bed
Sweat and tears start to rain
From the two visions in my head
The earth is pulsating rapidly with wind and rain
Any moment now the storm is due
Screams pour out of the sky
Down comes the pain
This one is new
The house is alert now
My husband at my rescue just in time
Holding in his hands was not thunder
But OUR fresh new bundle of
Pure sweet sunshine.
A baby girl!!

"Starting Over"

You caress my mental
Like the ocean shapes the sand
Electric currents passes through me
By the touch of your hand
Unparalleled love
Always hear from the dove
Before it rains
No more worries
Tears or doubt
Because DIVINE LOVE took my pain
Saved me
Gave me a new heart
New thoughts
Hungry to breathe again
Standing pure
My soul is ready to start
Meditation brings love
Peace
Wisdom
Into my heart

"Cease the Curse"

Boyfriend after boyfriend leaves you broken
hearted
You constantly look for everyone else to blame
Before the healing gets started
My body is young
But my mind is old
Raised by two teenage parents
I'm here to break this mold
She can't be alone
He is always in need
When I need to release all these emotions
I pick up the pen and let the ink bleed
Grandma does the best she can
Still she doesn't have to do it
Now cancer sticks ate up her lungs with cancer
Fluid
Actions are up and down
Balancing my life
Yet stable
I'd rather not have anything to do with you
Because you are not able
To speak to me
Without putting me down
I'd rather just sit here with my music
Peacefully
Don't bring your sword tongue around.

<u>Poem challenge! Write about your past relationship. Go!</u>

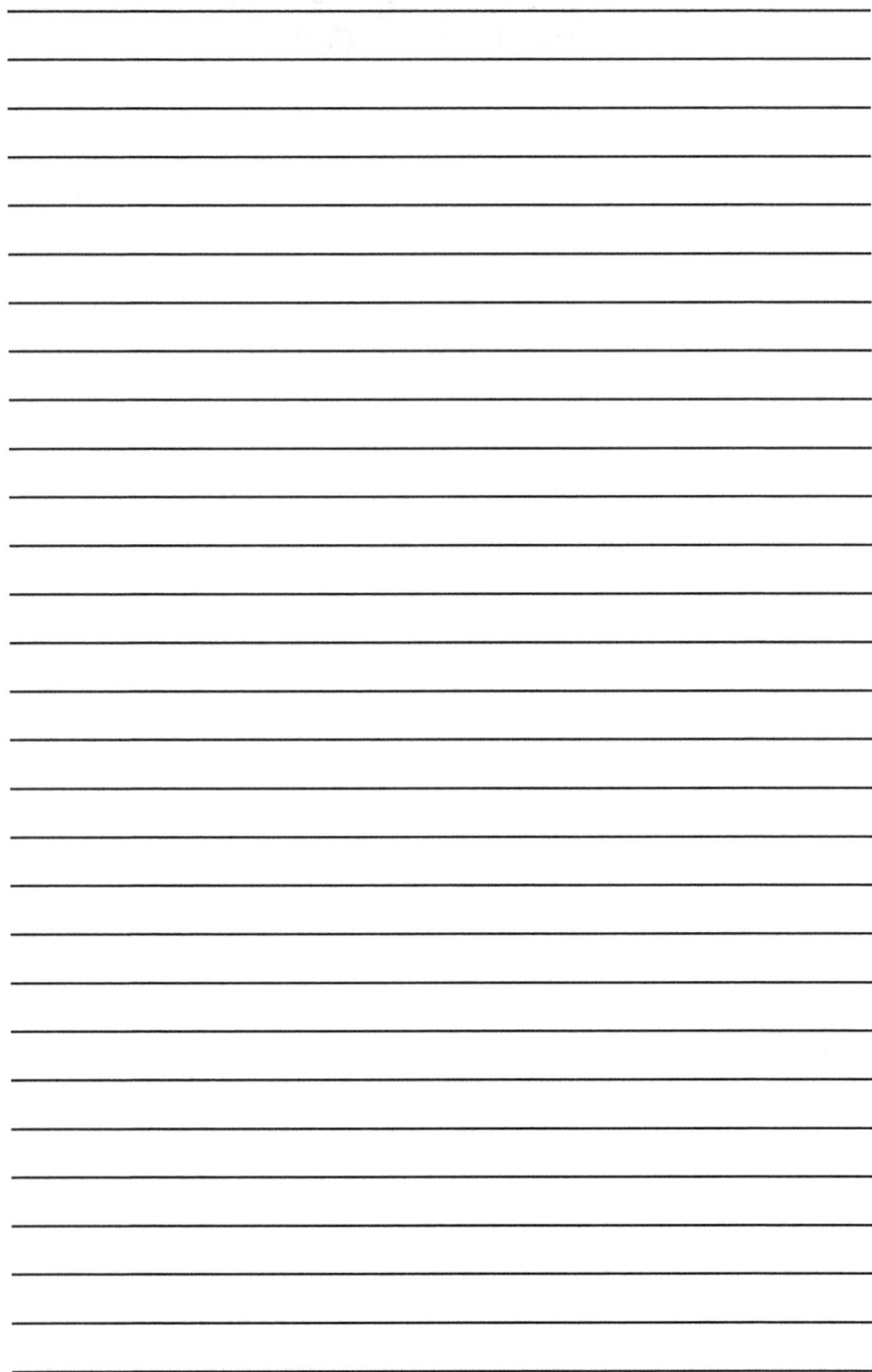

"Unprotected Thunder"

Selfish acts prolonged by those who choose
To abuse the love of others
Unwise to the game
Subtract themselves
Faking pregnant
Unwilling to be mothers
For misguided men who claim to be real
Simultaneously wanting to feel
The warmth of heaven
Ecstasy
Sunshine fills my eyes
Dazed
I'm speaking from my heart
Yet you still can't feel me
Your past is filled with hurt and despair
Hoping
Praying
Searching
Replacing
Trying to compare
Sexing
Riding
Smoking
Without a care
You love this one and that one
Wondering why life isn't fair
Never mind the words of others

LOVE YOU!
Don't go astray!!
Loving THE MOST HIGH
Will give you eternal happiness
Forever treasured you will stay!

What are some of your goals for self-improvement?

_____

_____

_____

_____

_____

_____

_____

_____

_____

_____

_____

_____

_____

_____

_____

_____

_____

_____

_____

_____

_____

_____

_____

_____

_____

_____

_____

"Caller I.D."

You are NOT the one
You played with my heart for fun
Now that I've moved on
The phone constantly rings
Surprised to know that I've been over you?
It only took one heartbreak for me, boo!
I thought you knew
How could you lie to me?
Your lover??!!
Wifey!?!?
Now, I won't pick up the phone
But YOU are still calling ME!?!?!?
(Had on my hip)
I am not the one
I smile now
Because YOU want ME back
As a matter of fact
I have someone who will love me forever
Something you will never understand
EXCUSE YOU!
I have a man!!!!

"MY REFLECTION"

Ever since you came into my life
I have more meaning now
When I look up I now have a reason to smile
It's not that I am insecure
Or that I have lack of love for self
It's just hard to define my reality
When I have no help
Ever since you came into my life
You helped me maintain
I don't have to say a word
And you are there!
It's so natural for me to love you
When you SHOW me how much you care
Ever since you came into my life
You filled that void that was my expanding in my heart
My eyes tear up
My breath pants
At the thought of us being apart
Your love reminds me of my grandmother
She is now my ancestor on the other side
Ever since you came into my life
My heart beats a new rhyme!

"ACKNOWLEDGEMENTS"

There are so many wonderful GOD-sent people who are in my life right now and they have all helped in guiding me along my journey in their own special way. Thank you MOST HIGH for blessing me with this talent and for loving me unconditionally because without you I would be nothing. Mom, (Michelle Graves) thank you for being the strong woman that you are. You have taught me so much by your strength to pursue your dreams under any means. Your spirit is like no other. I watch you go from teenage mom to receiving your Masters in Social work from Clark Atlanta University. I will always love you no matter. Forever & always. Dad, (Anthony Johnson) thanks for being so down to earth and for explaining life in such simple words. You mean everything to me. Grandma, (Martha Stewart) you were my backbone when I could not stand on my own. You taught me business and you always make sure I was taking care of. I love you for that. Grandpa Joe, you are my guardian angel. Thank you for teaching me Spanish. You always kept everyone laughing with your jokes and kept everyone looking with your style. You were a hardworking man and I love you and miss you dearly. Granny Johnson, (Edna Mae

Johnson) You taught me how to love unconditionally. Your love, hugs and food always won over everyone's heart. You taught me so many virtues that I will teach my children. I was deeply hurt when you left in 1994, but I feel your spirit around me every single day. Auntie, (Sherri Baker) you was so fun to be with. You taught me how to make the best out of every situation. I love you and miss you. Whenever I miss you I just call your only daughter (Kassie Ann) and listen to her talk and I hear your laughter in her laugh. Madear, (Willie Mae Miller) you were so wise! You lived through the most trying times in America. I learned many things by just watching you! You make me proud of my Cherokee Native American heritage. I promise to never waste my time or live in vain. Jevon Frank, you came into my life when I lost so many things and people around me. You helped me bring my daughter into this world and I will always be grateful for that. I will love you always and forever on so many levels. I admire your constant hustle and your drive to always pursue your dreams. Watching you helped me stay focused on my dreams. I'm happy our daughter has you as her father. Lambert Sayles, our relationship goes deeper than just being cousins. We have a connection like brother and sister. I miss you every day because you are in Chicago and I am here in Atlanta. You so smart, handsome and fun. You taught me how to stand up for myself when we were younger and I will never forget that. Kassie Griggs, you are such a beautiful woman and I see you being a mother to your three boys. Your mom would be so proud of you. Stay positive and continue to follow your dreams. Malik Stewart, you are so unique. I love your ability to progress under any circumstance.

You are so talented! I know that you will accomplish whatever you put your mind to. Fatou Toure', thank you for standing up for me and up to me when no one else would. I'll never forget what a great friend you are to me and others around you. I love you! Shomari Simmons and family, you are a father now and I am so grateful you and your family was there for me. Thank you for using encouraging words during my time of difficulty. You and your family will always have special place in my heart. I love you! Dawn Axam, thank you for teaching me day after day the gift of dance. You are a beautiful person who has many different gifts. The day you pulled me aside and spoke into me, it changed my outlook on my life forever. I'll never forget that. I love you! Nicole Hickman and family, you guys are amazing. You all are definitely one in a million. You all are my family away from home. I love you! Torwa Joe, (Fiya Starta) girl you have an energy that is out of this world. I loved you like a sister I never had.

We had so much fun performing and creating dances and making costumes. I'll never forget our bond. I love ya! Reyna Whitehead, my cousin sister. I have watched you grow over the years and now you are a beautiful mother. I admire your constant drive to be the best! Our bond is unbreakable. I will always be here for you! I love you! Uncle Derek, I love you so much! No matter what happens in my life you are there whenever I call. You are so strong and determined. I love you for always being there for me. Dan Anthony Sims and family, to watch you go from my excellent math teacher to now husband, father and principle. I admire your strive for excellence, your effective communication and your leadership. You are such a leader to most and you taught me so much. I'll never forget you and your beautiful wife. I love you both! Wanita Woodgette, (D.Woods) you are amazing. You blew up on television while I became a mother. Our lives went in two different directions but I'll never forget the fun times we had up all night writing songs and coming up with master plans to take over this world. Thank you for always encouraging me to follow my dreams. I am so proud of you. Represent for the GET SOME CREW!! Anthony Wilson and family, thank you so much for allowing me to place my poems on music. Blaze Station has been such a creative

place for me to unwind and release on the mic.
You are a great example of a husband, father and
friend. I admire you for that. Kessonga Sands,
thank you for all your ideas, your support and for
believing in me. Great job on both book covers.
May The Most High continue to bless your life in
everyway! Keishon Kessee, thank you for helping
me during one of my most trying spiritual times.
You are so wise and creative. Whenever we get
together it is always a great time. I love you!
Natina & Ro Martins, you both have been there
for me when I thought I had no one. You both
have proved to me what true friends are and I am
so happy to be a part of your wedding in
Bermuda! Black Love Rocks! I love you both like
a sister and brother! Tri-Cities Magnet
Department, thank you for allowing me to
perform, sing and dance on your stage for the
first time. I am so proud to say that I am a
graduate of Tri-Cities High School Class of 1997! I
love you all and I will never forget you all. My
family in Muncie, Indiana, the Millers', Johnsons',
and Marshalls'. My family in Chicago, the Evans'
and Sayles'. My family in Waycross Georgia and
California, the Wesleys' and McGauley'. My family
here in Atlanta the Whiteheads', Griggs',
Stewarts' and Thomas. My family in Brooklyn
New York, the Franks', I love you all. All my
friends and associates and the AIU (buckhead

campus) family Mrs. Leggett-Taylor and Kinetra Watson Norwood. I could go on and on so if I forgot you please forgive me in advance. It was not intentionally. I love you all. Each of you have touched me in many different ways. This is just the beginning of many books to come.
Ayana Johnson/Empress Yana Jay

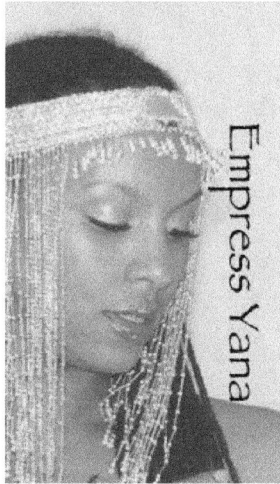

Www.EmpressLyfe.com for all upcoming performances and book signings.

www.ingramcontent.com/pod-product-compliance
Lightning Source LLC
LaVergne TN
LVHW051206080426
835508LV00021B/2837